A letter to the girls I've never met

A letter to the girls I've never met

Toochi Samsylvanus

*To those who inspired it,
and never got the chance to read it.*

*To my daughter and to my family,
leaving something for you to cherish forever.*

*To the girls who feel like they don't have a voice,
can't use it or haven't found it.*

*To all the girls in the world who are strong,
beautiful, intelligent & independent.
Greatness does not wait til you are ready.*

*And, to the girls and women who are first born
daughters, you're not alone and you're not unnoticed,
you're a diamond sitting on the tallest shelf.*

Contents

A letter to the girls I've never met

The eldest daughter

To describe myself to others,
I would use words of a definition:
A pathological people pleaser

Society often mistakes it for genuine kindness and
helpfulness,
But on the eldest daughter,
it is masked as *independent, stable,* and *empathetic.*
Which all happen to be qualities of parentification.

The title itself comes with its benefits,
like having the biggest role in everyone's lives.
Not just within the family walls.
But outside the picture frame,
there's almost nothing more than the role of

A therapist.
A perfectionist.
A guardian.
And a back-bone.

Every skilled, satisfactory quality, you can think of,
the eldest daughter carries that embodiment
through & *within* her.

In my mother's eyes

In my mother's eyes, I see a love so strong
A love that stood so tall, in test of time
Through every up & down, every cheer & smile
Through every tear we've ever shed
In my mother's eyes I see a love that will never die

As I grew older, and time passed by
I began to see through my mother's eyes, the woman
behind a mother, the woman she used to be
All the dreams she ever had, the hopes she prayed for,
so deeply, the love she carried so close to her heart &
the love she gave... without a price

In my mother's eyes, I see the sacrifices she made for me
The love she gave,
and dreams she set free for mine to be achieved
In my mother's eyes, no other world I rather not be.

Unavailable

When presence is known but not possible
When presence is known but unreachable
When you try to speak up and make your voice known,
yet at an instance no one hears you.

You sit back & take a break in
and decide not to speak up again.
Even when they reach out to you.
You turn your head
and put your phone down.

And tell yourself you deserve a break from the world.
From all the things you know and don't know about.
From all the things your mother vowed to protect you
from, the minute you came into the world.

Now
Isolated in my room.
Late at night, at the edge of the bed.
Phone on silent with the do not disturb notification on.
Just like my mind, do not disturb and unavailable.

Me, myself and I

When I'm outside four walls,
in my own space, I feel at peace

No loud clashes, bangs or booms
No heavy tides coming up to choke me out and snatch
me with it
No random waves of sadness or distress,
waiting for me to give it a reaction

It's just me, myself and I.
Living in the present,
enjoying the moment as the trees dance side by side,
following each sync as the wind blows a cool breeze,
calming the air
and the birds fly in flocks, singing praises to the most high

Nothing can come in between this moment
of me and my peace, in this present space I share
with no one else but me, myself and I.

Escape the mindscape

This year, I've learned to fold it and keep it tucked away,
I've learned to pack all the nuisance in storage boxes
I've decided that the word "overthink"
should no longer be chained to my name or my mind

To prefer to be alone
in your own space
between the magnitudes of the mind and soul

Being settled here can be a blessing in disguise
but a curse slowly unfolding by the minute
You have peace of mind, at first
then the next you find yourself questioning,
any and everything, to ever exist or happen in your life

You begin to be socially lost,
Confused, and weary
trying to catch up with the world
outside your head,
out-running your thoughts
Thoughts that are ready to consume you

Only   In
the   The
Blank   *M   i   n   d*
Spaces   are the ones
                                              never filled.

The day I woke up

The day I woke up
Is the day I took a breath
The day I woke up by God's grace

The day I woke up
Was the day I officially realized
that anything in life is possible
The day I earned my biggest accomplishment
Also the day I learned that I can do anything I aspire

The day I woke up
It was the day he told me how much I meant to him
Through his words and his effort, he was the first
person that truly saw me for who I am

The day I woke up
Was the day I finally understood that
flashy, expensive cars, *real* shoes and bags that cost
thousands of dollars, trendy hobbies and clothes
Do not follow you to the grave
Earthy desires and materialistic things are just for
"the gram"
Not real life.

The day I woke up was the day I realized car accidents
can happen to anyone
Including me.

The day I woke up
It was the day my biggest fear came true
At 12:06 am PST on April 14th, 2025
The day my grandmother passed away
Was the day the world fell apart in my hands

Since that day I woke up, that was the day I finally
realized that
Time doesn't stop for a single soul
Even if you chased it all your life, as if your life were a
marathon
It will never stop.
Not a speck of it is spared, for anything or anyone in
this world, and never will be

But the day I take my eternal rest
Will be the day all my hopes and dreams come true
The day I come back home,
back to the hands of The Lord

In the sky, I can see

In the sky, I see it pictured so clear,
I can see the mansion I want to live in,
with my dream cars parked out in front

I can picture my dream job, and a big front yard
With a *huge* pool in the back
I can picture my *dream* closet
with all my fly outfits and my shoe collection
I can picture my very own library,
filled with books I'd *never* get bored of,
and a vinyl collection that could play for *days nonstop.*

I can see my own beautiful family, with my mom, my
sister and my best friend as my neighbors

But none of those things are real, at least not yet.
But when I look into the sky, they're not there.
That's because it's all a fantasy.
The sky is filled with nothing but shades of blue and air

In the sky, I can see my imagination go wild and run its
course
Just like my dream, my daydream

Divine alignment

I feel myself getting closer and closer.
Deeper and deeper, the more I do.
The more I say, the longer I commit.

In every word, I speak, more eyes look
and more heads turn.
Every step I take, more fear falls off my back.
Floors tremble, not because it's unstable,
but because I'm worthy of it.

The more movement I make, the more they watch.
Every sound I make, every word I say, the more
they listen.
Every idea I input, they observe. It almost feels like I'm
being watched like a TV show.
But.

I'm watched, not because they think I'm "cool".
I'm watched, not because they want me to disappear.
I'm watched, not because they're envious of my every
move.
I'm watched, not because they've sent distractions
from my enemies.
I'm watched, not because they, themselves, are
monitoring spirits that follow me.

But really.
I'm watched because I have everything they don't.
I'm watched because
I've been placed under divine alignment.

The meaning of divine alignment is
to be in the state of being in harmony with a higher
power's plan or will.

Like *honesty* and *trust*, going hand in hand.
And by this alignment placed over me.
I trust in the Lord's plan for my life.

Faith > Fear

No matter how much I try, even if I defeat fear,
it always comes, creeping back, like it never left.

Fear, and his cousin, *doubt*, are always trying to take
turns playing catch inside my mind.
Constantly compounding my thoughts.
In everything I say, do and think.

As fear falls off my back and lets go of my shoulders,
it always comes back.
And every time it does, knows where to look and what
to find.

When I break free from its chains, I always feel a sense
of relief.
Each time that is, I'm always starting over with my best
friend, *faith*.
It feels like I'm waging war between the two,
like when you have an *angel* in one ear,
and the *devil* in the other.

For as long as I have lived, my best friend, Faith.
Faith has always stuck around by my side.
And of course, it's always when fear is nowhere near.
When me and Faith hold hands, Hope opens the door
and dances towards me.

In that moment, I feel more connected, overjoyed and
safe.
Now love steps in, and my heart is profound, ready to
express my truest self.

Even with that, I've always watched my back around
fear.
The last time I let my guard down,
it had forsaken me, and left me alone with *Regret* and
his other cousin, *Shame*.
Since all this has passed and took its place,
I've lived,
I've learned
and I've grown.
And still am.

But now, I know what I want.
And I know what to do.
I've learned the strategies of fear and I've observed all
of his family members.
I've learned and I'm all geared up, ready for my fade
next time I see him.

Forever, I've acquired and now
I'll always choose *Faith* over Fear.

No text back?

Waiting on a text back
Buzzing tempts body's response
Still waiting on a text

Evolving

I can't let fear consume me
I won't allow shame to schedule a meeting
I refuse to let anxiety silence me
And I certainly won't accept defeat.

I can't allow my body to stay still, stuck in time because
realistically time does not stop.
It won't stop and will never stop.
That's what makes everything so confusing.
Humans can take as many breaks and "time outs" as
we want to, but really, when we say we need a break,
Does the clock ever stop?

The answer is simple.
No.
The clock never stops, not a millisecond, not ever by
accident.
It just keeps going and going. Like my list of tasks.
Sweep the floor, wash the dishes, water the plants,
clean my room, make dinner, do the laundry.
You get the point..

What I'm trying to say is.
It's okay to take a break,
we all need one because we're all human.
But don't allow a "break" to be an excuse to not achieve.
Don't delay yourself because you don't *feel* ready.
Of course, don't deny yourself *your* dreams just
because you're scared of them *actually* coming true.
Time will never wait til you're ready and neither will
your greatness.

"Greatness does not wait til you're ready."
Someone wise, once told me.
And I repeat it back to myself as I stand up to perform
my piece, and nothing to hold me back.

Love is lost

The way the world sees love, comes in many different
levels.
Some cases it begins with a follow, then a text or DM.
Then that leads to small talk and then a "link", by the
time you know it, it's over.
Back to square one.
Lust.

Then there's level two, the materialistic level.
Greed.
All the expensive gifts, sophisticated trips, overpriced
bouquets with a notecard, etc.
But underneath, all those fancy things.
When it fails, people *fail* to realize that,
There was nothing else other than all those
Gifts.
No real relationship. Just receipts.

I could go on and on about different types of
"relationships" the world has defined as "love".
The world itself has sucked away the true meaning of
love, & replaced it with temporary pleasures.

Now everyone is weary, lost & confused.
With no true love in their hearts.

Love is a losing game

You said I was special, and that you hold me close to your heart.
Naturally, I believed you, even when doubt lingered in my mind.

No matter how much I tried, nothing was ever enough.
And that's okay, because I'll go somewhere I am wanted.

Your imperfections never mattered, in my eyes.
You always seemed so strong and true.

I'll always wonder why you always left, but will forever question why you never stayed.

Love waits for me

Love's waiting for me
Uncertain how much longer
But love will be here

Absent

Physically.
Is when, he doesn't show up to big things that mean a
lot to you.
But he makes up for it by taking a picture, hours later.
That counts as something, right?

Emotionally.
Is when he walks by, every day, but almost no words are
spoken.
Maybe, I could survive off of a few good mornings now
and then, right?
Even through my struggles to express my emotions,
without getting angry and upset, at least I *try*. But
defensiveness & avoidance is easier.

Verbally.
How do you get to say what and where I can go?
How do you even get a say when you don't even care &
you're barely aware.
But I guess you do have the 'power' to do that, right?
Either way, it's not stopping me.

I still keep going, like I am going to arrive at the mall in 5
mins to see my friends.
Is the same way that life keeps going.
But your absence will still be here,
forever waiting on you.

To all the girls in the world

To the girl who feels alone, no matter how many friends she has and people she meets.

To the girl that understands what it means to talk too much, yet barely speaks a word.

To the girl that lost someone so close and dear to her heart, life is changing, in a weird way.

To the girl who is a mom, you're doing amazing.

To the girl that is the older sister but also the parent, it's not selfish to think and care about yourself.

To the girl that feels too much, sees too much and hears too much, I understand what it means to be the glue.

To the girl that struggles with her identity, be you no matter what.

To the girl that's scared of attention, you are worthy of being praised for being amazing.

To the girl that's scared to speak up, it's now or never and even if the outcome is bad, it doesn't define you or make you wrong.

To the girl that fell into peer pressure, trust yourself , be true and don't allow opinions to affect your values.

To the girl that's attached to him, love yourself and give yourself peace.

To the girl that is an overachiever, it's perfectly okay to take a break, we all need one.

To the girl that doesn't have a mother or father figure, they love you, even if they're not there to show it or to say it.

To the girl that isn't happy in her body, your body is beautiful and unique, why change it for something that's not real?

To the girl that struggles with her complexion, God blessed you with something so beautiful that people pay for.

To the girl that struggles to talk to her mom because of impossible standards, Be true. Stay authentic and reach your own goals.

To the girl that's scared to show her crown because it's not the beauty standard as yours is the opposite, don't be a star trying to fit in a circle.

To the girl that tries to tame her crazy, curly hair, let it out, be free and be authentically, you.

To the girl that misses her family, they're all in paradise watching over you.

To the girl that misses the way things used to be, change can be hard but it's a new beginning.

To the girl that feels too skinny or too fat, we are all beautiful in our own way, not every eye will perceive it but the right one will.

To the girl that convinced herself that it's okay, even when you said no, it's not okay and healing takes time.

To the girl that loves trust and honesty yet it offends you when it's presented, you'll live, learn and grow.

To the girl that loves affection yet can't accept it, one day your walls will fall for your good and worry will leave your heart.

To the girl that hides her dreams and aspirations because the time isn't right, time will never be perfect, it's now or never.

To the girl that's scared to pursue her career, you never know how far you'll go until you make the first step.

To the girl that struggles with keeping God at the center of your life, your effort shows and is what really matters, not perfection.

To all the beautiful girls in the world, you all matter, your stories, backgrounds, trauma, experiences, love, hate, insecurities, proud moments, achievements, disappointments, wins, losses, and battles, *All Matter.*

It all makes us each unique and beautiful in all the ways that we are.

Even if you *think* it doesn't :)

Acknowledgements

I'm so blessed to know and work with everyone that helped, guided, organized & advised me throughout my journey writing this book. I'm so very grateful to have such amazing leaders and support. First, I want to give God the glory for this amazing opportunity to write my first book, without him it wouldn't have been possible. I want to thank my mommy and my dad for being committed to taking me to class no matter how uncertain it was. I want to thank them for every sacrifice they've ever made for me. Thank you for sacrificing your dreams so mine could come true. I'm forever grateful & I love you.

To Mr. Brandon Allen, Thank you so much for having me a part of the Youth Writer's camp. You have made such a remarkable impact in my life and have taught me many things I'll never forget. Meeting you at the San Bernardino County Poetry Out Loud finals was truly a blessing in disguise. You've helped me grow not just in poetry and literary arts but as a person as well. I'm forever grateful for you and thank you for always believing in me and pushing me to believe in myself.

I want to thank Mr. Tellyer, my English teacher from sophomore year. Thank you for being a part of my journey in poetry. Even from little things like staying 5 more minutes to continue practicing and reciting poems, to big things like honoring me in important meetings and in front of lots of remarkable people in our community and educational world. You've never given up on me, always supported and encouraged me to do my absolute best. I'm so grateful to be known as one of your students and you are more than a student could ever ask for.

To my sister, Kelechi, and my brothers, Ihe and Ike. Thank you for being the best siblings I could ever ask for. No matter how imperfect we each are, our laughs, tears, jokes and memories are all important to me and I will forever cherish our bond. Thank you for encouraging me to follow my dreams and conquer my achievements, I love you guys, always.

I want to thank my family, my aunties and uncles for encouraging me to chase my dreams.
I want to thank all my English teachers I've ever had for encouraging me to continue writing.
Thank you to those that are close to me like some of my close friends, for always being there for me in so many ways true friends are.
Thank you to everyone that is or was a part of my life, you've made an impact on my life, whether it was big or small, negative or positive.

Lastly, I'm thankful for all my readers, whether you connected to any of my poems or not. If you liked my book or barely got through it. Thank you and I'm grateful to have you as a reader.

About the Author

Toochi Samsylvanus is a Nigerian-American 11th grade student, born and raised in Southern California. Toochi began writing poetry in 5th grade, after covid hit and rediscovered her talent later again in 8th grade. In 2025, she placed 2nd in her school-wide Poetry Out Loud competition, later went and placed 1st in the San Bernardino County POL finals, and made it to the state finals and won 2nd place in the whole of the state of California. Toochi's love for poetry has grown so impressively & beautifully and continues to shine.

youthwriterspress.com

A program of Youth Writer's Camp, Inc., Youth Writer's Press exists to create a safe space where young voices are heard, valued, and amplified. We are dedicated to producing and publishing work that allows youth to share their truths with the world. Our mission is to equip the next generation of writers with the resources, confidence, and platform to turn their stories into lasting works that resound far beyond the page.

youthwriterscamp.com

This book was created as part of Youth Writer's Camp, Inc., a nonprofit organization whose mission is to motivate communities to redefine hope for young people through mentoring, enrichment, and creativity.

In our workshops and programs, we blend literacy enrichment, social-emotional development, and creative entrepreneurship — using writing as a tool for healing, growth, and community connection.

Youth Writer's Camp Values:

COURAGE Creating the strength to face challenges with confidence.

RESILIENCE Creating the ability to bounce back and keep moving forward.

EMPATHY Creating connections by truly understanding others' feelings.

AUTHENTICITY Creating a space where you can be your true self without masks.

TRANSPARENCY Creating an atmosphere of openness and honesty, where vulnerability is valued.

ENTERPRISING Creating opportunities through innovation and a dynamic mindset.